History and activities of
Ancient Greece

Greg Owens

Heinemann

Essex County Council Libraries

 www.heinemann.co.uk/library
Visit our website to find out more information about Heinemann Library books.

To order:
☎ Phone 44 (0) 1865 888066
  Send a fax to 44 (0) 1865 314091
📄 Visit the Heinemann Bookshop at www.heinemann.co.uk/library to browse our
💻 catalogue and order online.

First published in Great Britain by Heinemann Library, Halley Court, Jordan Hill, Oxford OX2 8EJ, part of Harcourt Education. Heinemann is a registered trademark of Harcourt Education Ltd.

© Harcourt Education Ltd 2007
First published in paperback in 2008
The moral right of the proprietor has been asserted.

Editorial: Audrey Stokes
Design: Kimberly R. Miracle in collaboration with Cavedweller Studio
Picture research: Mica Brancic
Production: Vicki Fitzgerald

Origination: Chroma Graphics
Printed and bound in China by WKT Company Limited

13-digit ISBN 978 0431080857 (hardback)
11 10 09 08 07
10 9 8 7 6 5 4 3 2 1

13-digit ISBN 978 0431080932 (paperback)
12 11 10 09 08
10 9 8 7 6 5 4 3 2 1

British Library Cataloguing in Publication Data
Owens, Greg
Ancient Greece. – (Hands on ancient history)
1. Greece – Civilization – To 146 B.C. – Juvenile literature
2. Greece – History – To 146 B.C. – Juvenile literature
I. Title
938
A full catalogue record for this book is available from the British Library.

Acknowledgements
The author and publishers are grateful to the following for permission to reproduce photographs: Ancient Art and Architecture Collection, pp. **7**, **8**, **18** (C M Dixon), **26**; Art Directors and Trip, p. **20** (Helene Rogers); Bridgeman Art Library, pp. **6** (Museo Archeologico Nazionale, Naples, Italy), **14**; Corbis, pp. **11** (Araldo de Luca), **13** (Elio Ciol), **15** (Bettmann), **16** (Michael Nicholson), **17** (Yiorgos Karahalis/Reuters), **22** (Araldo de Luca); Harcourt, pp. **19** (David Rigg), **25** (David Rigg), **29** (David Rigg); NorthWind Pictures, p. **9**; Photo Scala, Florence, p.**12** (Courtesy of the Ministero Beni e Att. Culturali).

Cover photographs of an ancient Greek vase (foreground) reproduced with permission of Getty Images/ Bridgeman Art Library and Parthenon (background) reproduced with permission of Getty Images/ Photodisc.

The publishers would like to thank Greg Aldrete, Eric Utech and Kathy Peltan for their assistance in the preparation of this book.

Every effort has been made to contact copyright holders of any material reproduced in this book. Any omissions will be rectified in subsequent printings if notice is given to the publishers.

Contents

Some words are shown in bold, **like this.** You can find out what they mean by looking in the glossary.

Chapter 1: The world's first democracy

Greece is a country in southern Europe. It includes many small islands in the Mediterranean Sea. The first **civilization** in this area was the Minoans. They lived on the island of Crete. Many of their cities were destroyed in about 1450 BCE. Some scientists think that a volcano was to blame. Soon other cultures developed in Greece.

Ancient Greece was made up of many smaller settlements. Some were on the mainland and others were on islands. Mountains or water often separated these communities. Each small community was known as a city-state, or *polis*. Each city-state had its own laws. The city-states often fought with each other. Sometimes they banded together to fight outside forces. The most famous city-states were Athens and Sparta.

The ancient Greeks gave us many beliefs and ideas. One of the most important ideas was about government. Before the Greeks, most people were ruled by kings or small groups who held power over everyone. The Greeks created something new: a government where people had rights. In Greek society, people created their own laws. It was called **democracy**.

Timeline

1600–1100 BCE
Mycenaean civilization

479 BCE Greeks defeat invading Persians, ending the Persian Wars

338 BCE King Philip II of Macedon conquers Greece

2800–1450 BCE
Minoan civilization based on the island of Crete

750–490 BCE
Rise of independent Greek city-states and self-government

404 BCE
Athens falls to Sparta, ending Peloponnesian Wars

146 BCE
Greece becomes part of the Roman Empire

The phrase BCE means "Before the Common Era", a time before Christianity was a popular religion. The term BC is also used to mean the same thing.

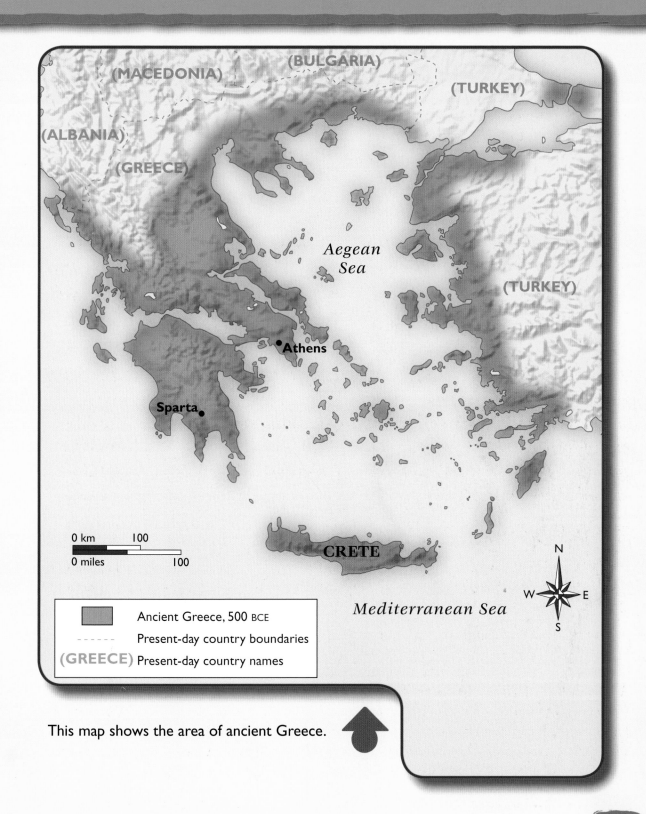

This map shows the area of ancient Greece.

Athens and Sparta were both city-states, but they were very different. The people of Athens were proud of their culture and knowledge. Spartans thought that strength and military power were most important.

Athens

Until 508 BCE, kings and rich landowners controlled Athens. There were strict rules about who could own land. A person who owed money could be forced to work as a slave. In 508, a leader named Solon passed new laws to change those rules. These changes made the government more democratic. The word **"democracy"** comes from two ancient Greek words – *"demos"* meaning "people" and *"kratia"* meaning "power". So, democracy means "people power".

Athens was divided into ten tribes. Fifty men from each tribe formed a group called the Council. The Council made all the laws. These laws had to be approved by the Assembly. The Assembly included all male **citizens** of Athens.

Solon was the leader who brought democracy to ancient Greece.

The *bouleterion* was the original meeting place of the Athenian council.

In court, any citizen could bring charges against another. Both the accuser and the accused spoke for themselves. There were no lawyers. The jury voted using circular tokens. A token with a hollow centre meant guilty. A token with a solid centre meant innocent.

A democracy did not mean that everyone was free. Women, slaves, and non-citizens had few rights. But it was the first time in history that people had the right to determine their own government.

The beginning of democracy

"The many were in slavery to the few, the people rose against the upper class. The strife was keen, and for a long time the two parties were ranged in hostile camps against one another, till at last, by common consent, they appointed Solon to be mediator and Archon (leader), and committed the whole **constitution** to his hands."

From *The Athenian Constitution* by Aristotle, written 350 BCE.

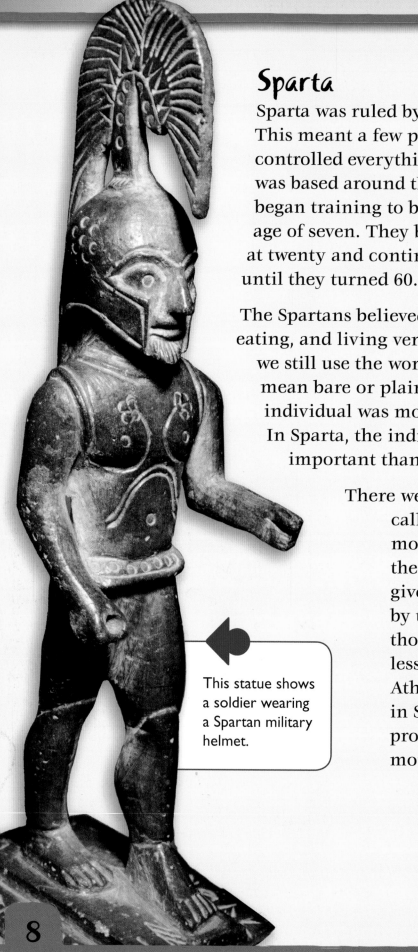

Sparta

Sparta was ruled by an **oligarchy**. This meant a few powerful people controlled everything. Spartan culture was based around the military. Boys began training to be soldiers at the age of seven. They began active duty at twenty and continued as soldiers until they turned 60.

The Spartans believed in dressing, eating, and living very simply. Today we still use the word "spartan" to mean bare or plain. In Athens, the individual was most important. In Sparta, the individual was less important than the state.

This statue shows a soldier wearing a Spartan military helmet.

There were slaves in Sparta called *helots*. They mostly worked on the farms that were given to the soldiers by the state. Even though Sparta was less democratic than Athens, women in Sparta owned property and had more rights.

War between Athens and Sparta

Athens and Sparta were the two most powerful city-states in the ancient Greek world. Although they fought together against foreign invaders, they remained enemies. Each tried to influence other city-states to live like them.

In 431 BCE, Athens and Sparta began a series of battles that lasted almost 30 years. This was known as the Peloponnesian War. When the war was over, Sparta conquered Athens and set up an oligarchic government. It was known as the Thirty Tyrants. Greek **democracy** survived a little bit in different city-states. But it was never as strong as it had been in Athens before the war.

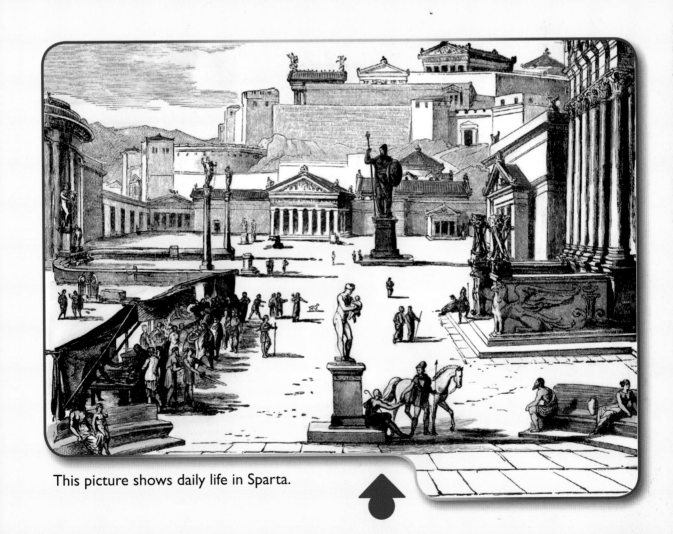

This picture shows daily life in Sparta.

Chapter 2: Life in ancient Greece

Most Greek houses were built with bricks. The bricks were made from mud that had been dried in the sun. The house was a big square with an open courtyard in the centre. The courtyard often had a well or a tank for the family's water supply. The walls of these homes were sometimes decorated with a type of painting known as fresco.

The Greek home was divided into the male area (*andron*) and the female area (*gunaikon*). Women did all the cooking and household chores, so the kitchen was part of the *gunaikon*. The *andron* was a room with several long couches. This was where men and their male friends enjoyed their time away from work or business.

Food and clothing

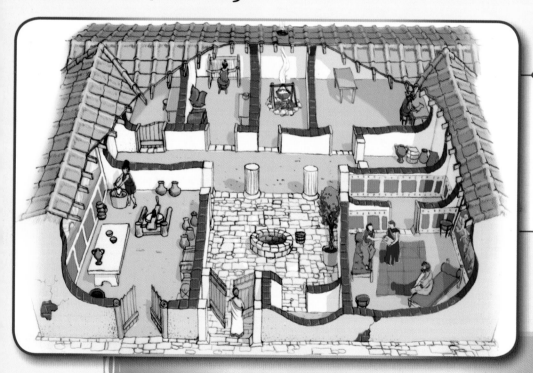

This illustration shows a typical ancient Greek home.

Oikos

The Greek word for house is *oikos*. From this came the word *oikonomia*, which means "household management". This is where the modern English word "economy" comes from. The word "ecology", which refers to the study of living things and their environments, also comes from *oikos*.

The two women shown in the centre of this vase painting are wearing the traditional Greek garment, the *peplos*.

The main piece of clothing worn by both women and men was a large rectangular piece of wool. It was wrapped around the body, then pinned at the shoulder and tied at the waist. For men, this garment was called a *chiton*. For women, it was called a *peplos*.

Wheat, wine, and olive oil were three main parts of the ancient Greek diet. People also ate grapes, figs, and sesame seeds. They had vegetables such as beans and peas. In the coastal areas they ate a lot of fish. Many ancient Greeks kept goats and either drank their milk or made cheese from it. They did not eat very much meat.

Children

Greek children were wrapped up tightly in blankets and carried around until they were almost three years old. They spent most of their time with their mothers. When they were old enough to run and play, they often played in the outdoor courtyard of their house.

One of the most popular games was called knucklebones. It was played by tossing small bones up in the air. Then you had to catch them on the back of your hand. Ancient Greek children also played with yo-yos and dolls. They had other toys made from terracotta pottery.

 This terracotta statue shows young people playing a game of knucklebones. It is from about 300 BCE.

There was no law in ancient Greece that said children had to go to school. Most boys were sent to school by the time they were seven years old. There were few schools for girls because parents believed girls should stay at home to learn to run the household. Most children went to school for three or four years and at least learned to read. Pupils from wealthier families went to school for up to ten years.

School was divided into three main categories. The first included the study of reading, writing, arithmetic, and literature. The second category was athletics. Wrestling, gymnastics, and other athletic activities were part of the school curriculum. Music was the third category. Students were taught to sing and play a stringed instrument called a lyre.

"Alphabet"

In 403 BCE, Athens adopted the official form of the 24-letter Greek alphabet. The English word "alphabet" comes from the first two letters of the ancient Greek alphabet — alpha and beta.

The Greek alphabet, shown here, has 24 letters.

The *agora*, or marketplace, in Athens was the original meeting place of the Council, and also where people gathered to meet or shop.

Work

Most ancient Greeks were farmers. They grew olives and wheat and made wine. They raised sheep and goats on dry, rocky land that got little rain.

Trade was important to the Greek city-states. The merchants who traded were a major group of Greek workers. Sailors who carried goods back and forth across the ocean were another important group of workers. There were also doctors, architects, bankers, fishermen, carpenters, athletes, teachers, musicians, and actors.

Up to half of the people in Athens at this time were slaves. Most slaves were people from other countries. Many were captured during wars and forced into slavery. They did everything from household chores to dangerous work in silver mines.

Religion

The ancient Greeks believed in twelve main gods and goddesses who lived on Mount Olympus. The Greeks had a set of myths, or stories, from the distant past. These explained the origins and history of their people and their world. The Greeks built many temples and made offerings and animal sacrifices. They hoped to get the gods to help them. Now when we study these stories of the ancient Greek religion, we often refer to it as **mythology**.

Olympian gods and goddesses

Zeus – king of the gods

Poseidon – god of the sea

Hades – king of the dead

Hestia – goddess of the hearth, or home

Hera – goddess of marriage, Zeus' queen

Ares – god of war

Athena – goddess of wisdom

Apollo – god of music and healing

Aphrodite – goddess of love and beauty

Hermes – the messenger god

Artemis – goddess of the hunt

Hephaestus – god of fire

Zeus was the king of the Olympian gods.

Chapter 3: Arts and sports

The ancient Greeks thought that **intellectual** and physical activities were both very important. They were the first people to put on plays in a theatre. The ancient Greeks also invented the Olympics.

Greek theatre

Every year, Athens hosted a religious celebration that lasted for several days. Thousands of people would gather in the Theatre of Dionysus. They watched plays based on Greek myths. These plays were huge productions. They often included dozens of actors, dancers, and musicians.

The Greeks invented a type of play known as "tragedy", which did not have a happy ending. The ancient Greek word "*tragoedia*" meant "goat song". They either called it tragedy because the actors wore goat skins, or because a goat was sacrificed before the show.

The Theatre of Dionysus hosted the great dramatic festivals of ancient Greece.

The tradition of the Greek Olympic games continues today. In 2004, the modern Olympics were hosted in Athens.

The Olympics

In 776 BCE, the ancient Greeks held the first athletic competition at Olympia, an area sacred to the god Zeus. They started having these competitions every four years. Men from all over Greece competed for the honour of their city-states. There was an olive crown that went to the winner.

At first, the ancient Olympics was just a one-day running event. It later developed into a five-day competition in running, jumping, wrestling, and javelin throwing.

Heraea games

The ancient Greeks did not allow women to compete in Olympic events. Married women were not even allowed to attend the Olympics. But there was an athletic competition just for women known as the Heraea Games. It was named after the goddess Hera, wife of Zeus. This competition happened every five years. Women competed in running and chariot races, as well as drama and music.

By doing the recipe and activities in this chapter you will get an idea of what life was like for people living in ancient Greece.

Recipe: sesame buns

Sesame seeds were one of the earliest food sources of the ancient world. Records of its use date back at least 4,000 years. The sesame plant was used for food, spice, oil, and even ink by ancient cultures in Assyria, China, and Egypt. In ancient Greece, soldiers ate sesame seeds as an energy food. Sesame seeds with honey were also served at ancient Greek festivals and weddings.

Warning!

An adult should always be present when you are cooking.

Make sure you read all directions before beginning the recipe.

Supplies
- 500 g whole wheat flour
- 250 ml of milk
- 125 ml of olive oil
- 3 eggs
- 1 teaspoon of crushed aniseed
- 1 teaspoon of salt
- 200 g of sesame seeds
- 250 ml of honey
- greased baking tray

People of ancient Greece enjoy a banquet in this scene from a vase painting.

1 Preheat the oven to 180 °C (356 °F)

2 Mix the salt and the crushed aniseed with the flour and add the olive oil and the eggs while you knead the mixture.

3 Add the milk, half of the honey, and half of the sesame seeds to the flour mixture.

4 Form the flour mixture into bun shapes and put them on a greased baking tray.

5 Make a small hole in the middle of each bun. Fill these holes with the rest of the honey and sprinkle them with the rest of the sesame seeds.

6 Bake for 40 minutes, or until they are golden brown.

Sesame buns
With a few simple ingredients, you can make these tasty sesame buns in about an hour.

Activity: Make a peplos

The primary piece of clothing for ancient Greek men and women was the *chiton*. It is often confused with the Roman toga, but it is different. The ancient Greeks mostly wore *chitons* made of wool. A *chiton* was worn long by women, short by children, and either long or short by men.

It is basically a tube of fabric slipped over the head, and suspended on the shoulders. A belt could be worn around the waist. The women's *chiton* was called a *peplos*. You can make your own out of a simple piece of cloth.

Supplies
- single bedsheet or similar-sized fabric
- safety pins
- belt, sash, or rope
- fabric glue or sewing materials (optional)
- fabric paint or markers (optional)
- Greek-style ribbon or binding (optional)

A

1. Fold the fabric in half. Reach your arms out side-to-side. Ask a friend to make sure the fabric is wide enough to reach from one of your elbows to the other. Also make sure it reaches from your forehead to your knees or ankles, depending on how long you want it to be. (See Picture A)

2. Fasten the fabric closed along the long edge to form a large cloth tube. An adult can help you sew the long edge closed, or use fabric glue or safety pins to close the edge. You can even leave the edge open and use the belt to keep it closed later.

3 If you have closed the long edge of the tube, turn it inside-out so the sewing or pins do not show. Slip the tube over your head so the top edge is just below your armpits. (See picture B)

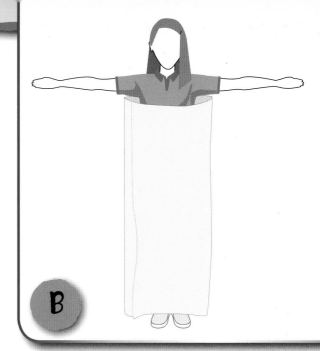

B

C

4 Ask a friend to help you bunch the fabric so that you can pull the front and back of it over each shoulder. Secure with large safety pins. These are the straps that hold the *peplos* onto your shoulders. (See Picture C)

5 Tie a belt, sash, or rope around your waist to hold the fabric in place and keep you comfortable. (See Picture D)

6 Now that you know how to wear your *peplos*, you could decorate the edges with a typical Greek pattern. You can use markers or paint to decorate it, or sew or glue ribbon or binding onto the *peplos*.

D

Peplos

This illustration shows what your ancient Greek *peplos* will look like when it is finished.

How would your wardrobe change if you had to make all of your own clothes?

Activity: make a Greek vase

One of the crafts for which the ancient Greeks are best known is their vase painting. There were two main kinds of vase painting. Black figure vases showed people or objects in black against a red background. Red figure vases were just the opposite. This activity will show you how to make your own painted Greek vase.

Supplies

- newspaper and/or white paper towels
- masking tape
- papier-mâché paste (high-cellulose mix)
- large bowl for making papier-mâché
- balloon
- cardboard tube: toilet tissue roll size for small balloon, large wrapping paper roll size for larger balloon
- thick cardboard cut into disc, larger in diameter than the cardboard roll
- pencil
- drawing paper
- paint and brush
- non-toxic acrylic varnish (optional)

Note: For a stronger vase with less drying time, use plaster gauze (available from craft shops) dipped in water instead of the newspaper strips and papier-mâché.

 This ancient Greek vase painting shows a group of women running.

1 Inflate the balloon and tie it closed.

2 Cut off about 5 centimetres of the cardboard tube. Tape this piece securely to one end of the balloon. Repeat this process, cutting another, longer piece of tube and taping it to the other end of the balloon. Tape the cardboard disc to one of the tubes. This will be the base of your vase. (See Picture A)

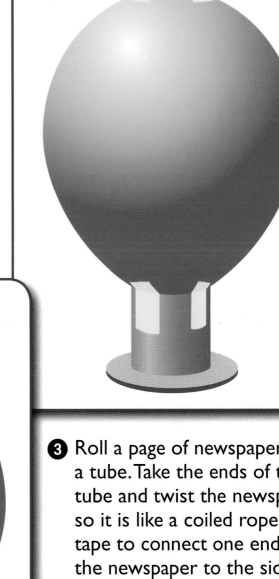

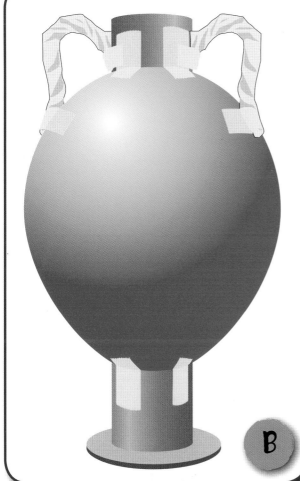

3 Roll a page of newspaper into a tube. Take the ends of the tube and twist the newspaper so it is like a coiled rope. Use tape to connect one end of the newspaper to the side of the balloon, and connect the other end to the cardboard tube on the top of your balloon. This is one of the handles. Repeat this process to make a second handle so both sides of the jar match. (See Picture B)

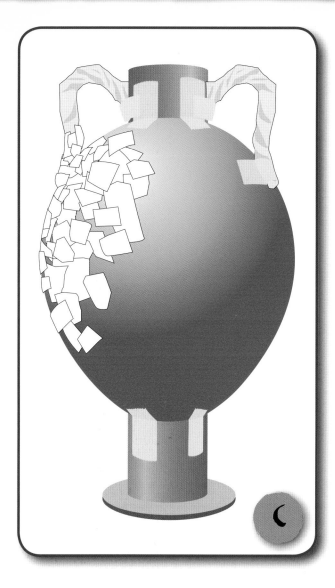

4 Make sure that everything is taped securely.

5 In a large bowl, mix the papier-mâché paste, according to the package directions.

6 Tear the newspaper into 2.5 centimetre-strips. Dip the newspaper into the paste, covering both sides. Pull the newspaper through your fingers to remove the excess papier-mâché. Carefully lay the strip onto the balloon, starting at the base and working your way up to the top. Extend it over the masking tape and cardboard pieces. Continue dipping and placing strips onto the balloon, covering it and the cardboard and the handles with an even layer. (See Picture C)

7 Cover the entire vase at least three times with papier-mâché. When you reach your last layer, you could use strips of paper towels instead of newspaper, so that your vase is white and easy to paint when it dries. Use a pencil to write your name on a piece of paper towel and paste it onto the balloon so you know which vase is yours when it dries overnight.

8 When the vase is dry paint it white (unless it is white already).

9 On a piece of drawing paper, sketch your ideas for the vase's decoration.

10 Use your pencil to draw your design on the vase. Paint your design carefully. When it dries you can make the paint shiny by covering it with acrylic varnish or white glue.

Greek vase

This is what a home-made painted vase looks like when it is finished.

You could show an athlete, or heroic person, or character from Greek mythology. What are some modern ideas you might choose for a design?

Activity: make a fresco painting

Fresco is a type of painting style that was invented by the ancient Greeks. These paintings were done on plaster walls while the plaster was still wet. This made the colours of the painting very bright. The ancient Greeks painted frescoes on the walls of their temples and houses for decoration.

Warning!

Read all directions before beginning the project.

An adult is needed to use the craft knife.

Supplies

- cardboard box
- pencil and paper
- ruler
- clear sticky tape
- cutting mat
- craft knife
- newspaper
- thick cord, string, or rope
- paint
- plaster
- poster paints
- paint brushes
- container for mixing plaster

Fresco painting was invented by the ancient Greeks. This fresco shows a warrior and his horse.

① Draw a design for your fresco.

② When you are happy with your design, use the cardboard to make a mould the same size. The sides should be five centimetres deep. Ask an adult to score the sides with the craft knife and turn them up. Tape the sides together to form a box. (See Picture A)

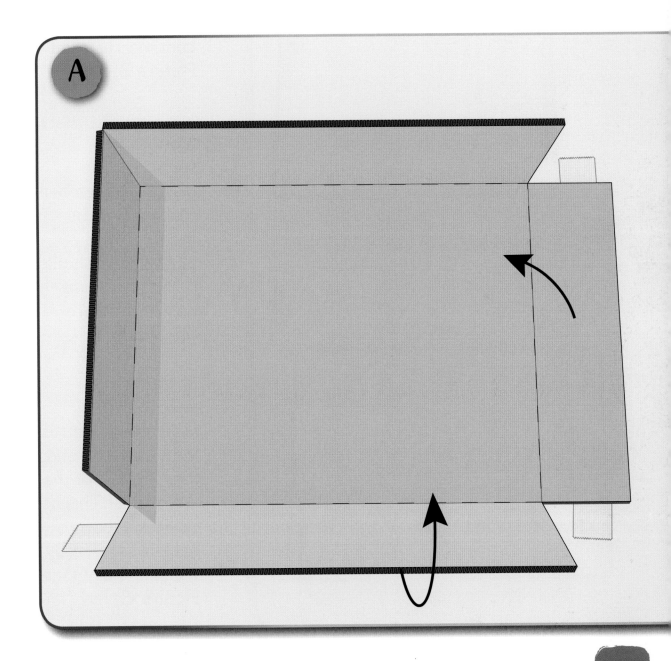

A

B

❸ Follow the directions on the container of plaster for mixing it. Then pour the mixed plaster into your mould to a depth of three centimetres. (See Picture B)

❹ Smooth the surface of the plaster. Remember that you will be drawing on the plaster so it should be as smooth as possible. Before the plaster dries, cut some cord or string into a piece that is fifteen centimetres long. Push the ends into the top of the wet plaster. This creates a loop to hang the fresco by when it is dry. (See Picture C)

5 When the plaster is dry, carefully remove it from the mould. Use a pencil to draw your design on the smooth surface of the plaster.

6 Use the poster paints to paint your design.

What kinds of designs would be appropriate in your house? What about in a Greek house?

Fresco

This fresco painting was made using the instructions on the previous pages.

Glossary

citizen person who lives in a town or city

civilization literature, traditions, customs, religion, and physical structures of a particular people at a particular place in time

constitution written record of the set of laws that govern a state or country

democracy system of government in which all people have the power to decide how they will live

mythology study of the myths, or stories, that different cultures tell to explain their origins and the world around them

oligarchy system of government in which a few powerful individuals control everything

More books to read

Arts and Crafts of the Ancient World: *Ancient Greece*, Ting Morris (Watts Publishing, 2006)

Excavating the Past: Ancient Greece, Christine Hatt (Heinemann Library, 2004)

Understanding People in the Past: the Ancient Greeks, Rosemary Rees (Heinemann Library, 2006)

You are in Ancient Greece, Ivan Minnis (Raintree Perspectives, 2004)

The instructions for the crafts and activities are designed to allow pupils to work as independently as possible. However, it is always a good idea to make a prototype before assigning any project so that pupils can see how their own work will look when completed. Prior to introducing these activities, teachers should collect and prepare the materials and be ready for any modifications that may be necessary. Participating in the project-making process will help teachers understand the directions and be ready to assist pupils with difficult steps. Teachers might also choose to adapt or modify the projects to better suit the needs of an individual child or class. No one knows the levels of achievement pupils will reach better than their teacher.

While it is preferable for pupils to work as independently as possible, there is some flexibility in regards to project materials and tools. They can vary according to what is available. For instance, while standard white glue may be most familiar, there might be times when a teacher will choose to speed up a project by using a hot glue gun to join materials. Where plaster gauze is not availabe, papier mâché can often be used. Likewise, while a project may call for leather cord, in most instances it is possible to substitute plastic rope or even wool or string. Acrylic paint may be recommended because it adheres better to a material like felt or plastic, but other types of paint would be suitable as well. Circles can be drawn with a compass, or simply by tracing a cup, roll of tape, or other circular object. Allowing pupils a broad spectrum of creativity and opportunities to problem-solve within the parameters of a given project will encourage their critical thinking skills most fully.

Each project contains a question within the directions. These questions are meant to be thought-provoking and promote discussion while pupils work on the project.

Index